# tranny trippin'

t. kilgore splake

TRANSCENDENT ZERO PRESS
HOUSTON, TEXAS

Cover design by Mutiu Olawuyi

ISBN: 978-1-946460-45-5

# tranny trippin'

t. kilgore splake

## Publisher's Introduction

splake journeys through the most passive reaches of the human mind, drawing at first triplets of poesy and finally longer splake-styled verse. When I refer to passive I mean these are memories, and memories are re-lived. As the Dutch philosopher Kierkegaard once quipped, "Life is lived forward, but understood backwards." Is poetry a way toward understanding the past or is it likely the closest thing to time travel we have?

The opening quotes make clear that "tranny" is not referring to the slur, but rather to transmission. The title opens doors to transgressive potential. As you visit the poetry, you may find the opening quote paralleling the work: "nameless terror yet too haunting and beautiful." Readers familiar with this bard of Calumet know the easy fusion of Beat with beauty's homage he presents.

--Dustin Pickering

kerouac road wisdom

"dreams were so irrational, so gray with nameless terror and yet too so haunting and beautiful"

"there was nowhere to go but everywhere, so just keep on rolling under the stars"

"our tattered suitcases were piled on the sidewalk again. we had longer ways to go. but no matter, the road is life"

"i was surprised, as always, by how easy the act of leaving was, and how good it felt. the world was suddenly rich with possibility"

"because in the end you won't remember the time you spent in the office, or mowing your lawn. climb that goddamn mountain"

writing today


mother's bel-air red lined

flying down narrow rural roads

without flat tire or deer crossing

# # # #

wilderness ghosts

early timber camps without cemeteries
serious epidemics killing young children
spirits resting in pine tree shadows

# # # #

au sable river ghost


hands holding fly rod
pen scribbling words on  blank page
jim harrison fishing for poems

# # # #

hangover

men's faculty bathroom
before early morning lecture
putting on professor face

# # # #

fats chuck berry elvis

ear buds twenty-four seven
lost in 50's vintage rock and roll
reincarnated teenage years

# # # #

ww-ii memories

mother angry at camouflage cap
worried another generation
preparing to fight new war

# # # #

illusions

free will to make decisions
forgetting ghosts in shadows
jesus mother american flag

# # # #

creativity

cool fluorescent light
soft quiet electric energy
no heat of raging flames

# # # #

mba college electives

swimming pool and lawn care
golf putting green techniques
finding cheap new car polish
making spreadsheet lies true

# # # #

morning with the muse

espresso steam rising
unlit cigarette in lips
holding pen tightly
staring at blank page
waiting for river of ink

# # # #

untitled

weekend writing workshops
conference literary panels
committees on publishing writings
not realizing imagination
comes from artist
creative work done alone

# # # #

perfecta win


caitlin drew blood sample

amber phoned medical results

emilie served morning espresso

elizabeth bagged groceries

laurie stamped out going mail

bukowski eat your heart out

# # # #

beyond loneliness


writer tired of living
desperate and hopelessly lost
in la dolce shadows
fellini's young waitress
gentle voice whispering
to new artist friend
save yourself come with me

# # # #

poetry is life

with creative freedom
no borders or limits
touching tasting reality
seeing and feeling
working outside of time
something many writers
don't understand

# # # #

rebirth

young woman's body
rising from brautigan creek
wet naked flesh
fresh from first sex
confidently walking
through wilderness shadows
moving to new life

# # # #

choices

graying senior remembering
always wanting to write poetry
paint sing or play guitar
after years quickly passing
words pictures songs
more important than
sports medals and ribbons
dusty school team trophies

# # # #

last chapter

artist's sudden death
prevented writing final poem
describing failing body
sadness of losing creative live
dying with personal dignity
like many people
mistakenly believing
life last forever
until shit happens

# # # #

surrender

will fight no more forever

chief joseph


reaching moment in life
when nothing left to do
at least feeling comfortable
finished creative projects
time to take it easy
which is fine for people
satisfied with themselves

# # # #

enjoying outdoors

escaping to wilderness
expensive recreational vehicle
easy camping comfort
like living at home
stove with oven
small air-conditioner
portable gas grill
for barbeque dinner
camp site american flag
green artificial turf
just like grass

# # # #

finding home

staring outside
coffee shop window
small village community
out of season quiet
dark highway miles
disappearing into night
café well lighted
warm place to stay
where nothing important
exciting things happening
poet feeling he belongs
deciding to stay

# # # #

goddamn independent

quiet unknown poet
without media representation
wikipedia or facebook connections
computer personal site
determined just to write
not discouraged by criticisms
or seriously care
if others read your poems
continuing walking the walk
after later creative writings
hoping to soon begin
talking the talk

# # # #

becoming a poet

for sylvia p.


from 'band nerd' t-shirts

to high school teenage sex

graduating to college campus

safe academic world

taking english classes

determined to write poetry

constantly struggling

to do serious writing

find right words

brain and blank page empty

as long as father

paying the bills

# # # #

modern education

hospital slap on the bottom
violent entry into world
learning abc's
counting to one hundred
adding and subtracting
figuring social security
medicare benefits
reading fine print
blue-cross insurance policy
understand assisted living
warehoused with others
,357 solution
hidden under pillow

# # # #

free at last

no longer caring for
girl friend's personal  problems
suffering with depression
sadly trapped in sadness
now free from grief trip
with positive view of life
chasing creative dreams
attempting to make art
leaving behind
broken hearted romance
hoping lover coping
wrestling with her demons
staying alive

# # # #

moving beyond ordinary

catholic school classes
"good morning sister"
boy scout oath
promising to obey god
boot camp private
rigid 'yes sir'
creating young rebels
beatniks and hippies
outlaw artists creating
novels poems paintings
writing songs making movies
wild avant garde art
revealing real life
making people think

# # # #

grocery shopping

large obese lady
flesh bulging in stretch pants
extra-large black t-shirt
with nike logo across front
"just do it' swoosh
grocery cart sacks
cans-r-us dollars
buying weekend refills
twelve-packs of cheap beer
relaxing woman's mind
for watching television
'lilias yoga and you'
imagining exercise motions
firming inner thighs

# # # #

small town dreams

another boring weekend
small midwestern village
dull bumfuck nowhere
with nothing to do
certain exciting things
in larger towns
farther down the highway
back corner table
three rivers truckstop
drinking cups of black coffee
creamers and sugar packages
next to napkin box
watching sixteen wheelers
filling tanks with diesel
turning back into dark night
driving to new worlds
leaving us behind

# # # #

relationship

pretty young girl
stroking gray beard
gently touching cheeks
warmth comforting artist
wearing faded jeans
sweat-stained black beret
deep wrinkled face
blurry eye sight
rapidly going deaf
loving aging writer
with quiet wild passion
deep feminine soul
knowing they must hurry
time being together
writing new poems
very important
with rat bastard time
tomorrow may never come

# # # #

# AUTHOR BIO

t. kilgore splake (born thomas hugh smith, december 8, 1936) is an american poet and photographer.

T. Kilgore Splake is a lifelong Michigander. He was born and raised in a family where paternal expectations were strong for the children to advance as far as possible into the corporate career wing of the nation's budding Military Industrial Complex. Striving to be ever the good son, he attained his B.A. and M.A. collegiate degrees from Western Michigan University in Kalamazoo , Michigan . He then felt his inner self start to tread water while he moved obligingly onward through a career as a high school and college professor. It was a career which included a 25-year stint at Kellogg Community College in Battle Creek , Michigan , where he taught Political Science. It was also a career that featured two troubled marriages that failed and difficult battles with demon rum ethers.

Upon turning forty years old, he began dealing with the restlessness of knowing more was "out there" and more was waiting to be uncovered inside himself. At that point, Splake began embarking on occasional, distinctively planned cross-country and Canadian road trips. He thus began to realize that the general malaise and discontent with "Society's Plan" instilled into him by his upbringing was much the same thing as written about (and written against) by the Beat Generation writers. The road led Splake to an epiphany, at the age of 44 and living out of a Ford Bronco. One morning over a hangover and a cup of coffee, he started writing. Ten years later the state of Michigan began discussing his potential early release from college teaching duties. Thomas Hugh Smith told the state of Michigan to send him a retirement check every month and T. Kilgore Splake was born,

After decades of dedication to his creative energies, Splake remains a legendary creative figure in the small press publishing world and an icon in the international underground poetry scene. He has written over 75 books of poetry and prose. He has composed four books of photography and over a dozen audio/video tapes, CDs, and DVDs. Additionally, his poetry and photography are eagerly sought after by other editors and publishers of anthologies, literary magazines, and art journals, where over 2,500 of his poems and photographs have appeared. He is also an often reviewed and interviewed artist in various blogs and websites from all around the Cyberspace World.

Splake was the founding editor of CLIFFS Soundings, a trailblazing international blend of writing and art that was published quarterly for five years, until his personal creative genesis started shifting to emotionally grueling memoir projects and heart surgery forced him to realize that time was of the essence.

Splake's work has earned him numerous Pushcard Prize nominations and drawn international attention to the Upper Peninsula of Michigan, his home base for over twenty years Up in the Cliffs, at the top of the Copper Keweenaw Peninsula, Splake maintains a Poet's Tree monument topped by a Tibetan Prayer Flag that draws international interest from visiting poets and artist hikers.

His work is archived at the University of New York/Buffalo , Ohio State University , Northern Michigan University , and Michigan Technological University . His books Sadness of Backwater Women and Last Train Out are part of the curriculum in poetry classes at Gogebic College in Ironwood, Michigan .

Thought Splake was blessed with several powerful romances upon embarking full-time into his writing life, age differences between he and the young women, along with other life circumstances, caused the disintegration of those love affairs. What is left to be told of those relationships can be drawn by the reader's intuition upon witnessing Splake's tattoos.

www.ingramcontent.com/pod-product-compliance
Lightning Source LLC
Chambersburg PA
CBHW060429090426
42734CB00011B/2502